S0-CBK-109

SPIDEROLOGY

SPIDEROLOGY

by Michael Elsohn Ross

photographs by Brian Grogan • illustrations by Darren Erickson

Carolrhoda Books, Inc. / Minneapolis

To Alec and Carrie and their pet spiders

Many thanks to Carl Brownless and the students at El Portal
Elementary School, California, and the students of Third Ward
School, Griffin, Georgia

Additional photographs courtesy of: © Steve Foley/Independent Picture Service, pp. 3, 11, 20;
© Robert and Linda Mitchell, pp. 6, 29, 30, 31, 33.

Text copyright © 2000 by Michael Elsohn Ross
Photographs copyright © 2000 by Carolrhoda Books, Inc.
Illustrations copyright © 2000 by Carolrhoda Books, Inc.

All rights reserved. International copyright secured. No part of this book may be reproduced,
stored in a retrieval system, or transmitted in any form or by any means—electronic, mechanical,
photocopying, recording, or otherwise—without the prior written permission of Carolrhoda
Books, Inc., except for the inclusion of brief quotations in an acknowledged review.

This book is available in two editions:
Library binding by Carolrhoda Books, Inc., a division of Lerner Publishing Group
Soft cover by First Avenue Editions, an imprint of Lerner Publishing Group
241 First Avenue North
Minneapolis, MN 55401 U.S.A.

Website address: www.lernerbooks.com

Library of Congress Cataloging-in-Publication Data

Ross, Michael Elsohn, 1952–
　　Spiderology / by Michael Elsohn Ross ; photographs by Brian Grogan ;
illustrations by Darren Erickson.
　　　　p.　cm.—(Backyard buddies)
　　Includes index.
　　Summary: Describes the physical characteristics and habits of spiders and
provides instructions for finding, collecting, and keeping spiders.
　　ISBN 1-57505-387-X (lib. bdg. : alk. paper)
　　ISBN 1-57505-438-8 (pbk. : alk. paper)
　　1. Spiders—Juvenile literature. 2. Spiders—Experiments—Juvenile literature.
[1. Spiders. 2. Spiders as pets. 3. Pets.] I. Grogan, Brian, 1951– ill. II. Erickson,
Darren, ill. III. Title. IV. Series: Ross, Michael Elsohn, 1952– Backyard buddies.
QL458.4.R668 2000
595.4'4—dc21   98-51406

Manufactured in the United States of America
2 3 4 5 6 7 – JR – 06 05 04 03 02 01

Contents

If, like a spider, I could spin,

I would dine outside, not in,

deftly trapping each flying treat,

silently sipping my silken sheet.

Like most folks, you have probably seen spiders before. Perhaps you are aware that they spin webs, but what else do you know? Have you ever taken time to introduce yourself to a spider?

Though there are a few spiders, such as the black widow, that can give you a painful bite, most spiders are harmless. It is rare for spiders to attack people. What people think are spider bites are usually the bite marks of insects such as fleas, kissing bugs, or mosquitoes. Despite this, many adults have arachnophobia (uh-RACK-nuh-FOH-bee-uh), or fear of spiders. These adults do their best to make kids afraid of spiders too. But there is no need for you to panic. Unless you are a small bug, there is nothing to fear from most spiders. Though many people fear spiders, it is spiders that are in danger of being harmed by giants like us. Be a gentle giant and handle spiders with care.

Sociologists study people, dendrologists investigate trees, and spiderologists spy on spiders. To be a spiderologist, all you need is a curiosity about spiders. Enjoy your journey into the world of the spider!

Welcome to Spiderology

Spider Hunt

Few things are more beautiful than a sunlit spiderweb. To find most spiders, all you need to do is scan the backyard or even the ceiling for silken webs. Though all spiders spin silk, not all kinds build webs. Some types of spiders can be found wandering about on plants or inside your home.

Web-building spiders may spend most of their lives in the same spot, so you can come back to webs you come across. Just keep notes on where you found the web. You might even make a map of the different webs around your home.

For closer study, a spider can be collected in a plastic container. Simply place the container in front of the spider and gently steer it in with a stick or pencil.

Before prancing into your home with a collection of spiders, consider how your family members might react. They may have a slight case of arachnophobia. To soothe any possible fears, you may want to read them the following article from the make-believe newspaper *The Torchlight Times.*

TORCHLIGHT Times

Caleb and Katie Carpenter of Opportunity, Montana, wanted a spider of their own. During a ski vacation at Big Sky, they had bought a charming book called *Charlotte's Web* about a very nice spider. Unfortunately, Mr. and Mrs. Carpenter were deathly afraid of spiders and vacuumed up any that were bold enough to enter their home. One day, Katie discovered a delicate little spider spinning a lovely web inside her bedroom. When her parents finally noticed it, Katie and Caleb begged them to leave it alone.

"It catches flies and keeps us from watching TV. We like it!" they exclaimed. "See how pretty it is?"

Mr. Carpenter did admit that he thought it was kind of cute, and Mrs. Carpenter, who didn't like flies either, thought the spider might be helpful. After months of sharing their home with a spider, the Carpenter kids are happier and their parents are a bit braver about web-spinning critters.

Like innkeepers of old, you can host a spider in your home. Give it a comfortable place to stay and some food to dine on. Though spiders can't pay for lodging, they do make nice guests. To house one, gather the materials below.

Inn Construction:

1. Make a layer of soil 2 to 3 inches deep in the bottom of the container.

2. Stick the branches upright into the soil. If your spider is a web spinner, it may attach its lines to the branches. If it is a free-roaming spider, it can use the branches for climbing.

3. Drop the spider in.

4. Pour a bottle cap of water into the inn every few days to keep the soil moist, but not soggy.

5. Add live insects, such as grasshoppers or flies, for the spider to catch for food.

6. Post a sign announcing that your container is a Spider Inn, so no one will be surprised if they look inside. Make sure you keep the lid on, so your spider doesn't wander.

7. Keep your inn away from direct sunlight. Clear containers can get as hot as greenhouses if left in the sun.

8. After you have had enough time to watch your guest, set it free outdoors.

You will need:

✔ a spider
✔ a large jar or other see-through container (with a lid that has tiny holes in it)
✔ some small branches
✔ moist soil
✔ a bottle cap
✔ live insects

Some innkeepers entertain themselves by keeping track of the activities of their visitors. They may discuss when they come in each night or what they order for breakfast. Like a nosy innkeeper, you too can watch your guests for unusual behavior.

Nosy Innkeeper

Check your spider at different times of the day to see what it's up to. Did it make a web? Is it more active at one time or another? What happens when you drop a bug into the inn? Does the spider seem to notice when you stare into its home? Keep a notepad near the inn so you can record your observations. Challenge your friends and family to discover secrets about your guest.

Your spider might get a little cramped staying in its inn all day, especially if it's the kind of spider that doesn't build a web. Give it a chance to roam by designing a spider jungle gym for it to play on.

Spider Jungle Gym

You will need:

✔ a spider
✔ a plastic dish tub
✔ a plastic bag or clear sheet of plastic for a lid
✔ toys such as mini-cars, balls, or dolls
✔ sticks and yarn
✔ anything else you can think of

What to Do:

In the dish tub, arrange the toys, sticks, yarn, and any other objects you find. Drop your spider into the tub and place the lid on top. Watch what the spider does. Does it climb anything? Does it like one place more than another? Now pretend you are a huge creature like a dinosaur. (To a spider you really are big!) Move your hand above the spider. Does it notice you? Say something to it. Does it react to the sound of your voice or to any other sounds?

Let it play for a while before returning it to the Spider Inn. It will be safer in its inn than wandering around your house.

Are you aware? Would you notice if your neighbor got a pet elephant? Would you have a clue if your best friend grew three inches overnight? Do you pick up on small details? Whatever your answers, the Aware Dare is for you. If you are completely tuned out, this game will help you tune in to picky little details. Being tuned in is extremely helpful when you are becoming familiar with new friends, such as spiders. On the other hand, if you are totally aware, this game will allow you to show off your sharp wits. Though it can be played alone, the Aware Dare is more challenging with two or more players.

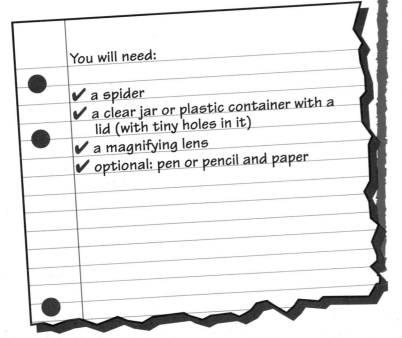

You will need:

✔ a spider
✔ a clear jar or plastic container with a lid (with tiny holes in it)
✔ a magnifying lens
✔ optional: pen or pencil and paper

How to Play:

1. Place a spider in the jar, and put on the lid.

2. Decide who is going to go first.

3. Beginning with player number one, take turns looking at the spider with the magnifying lens and sharing observations. For example, someone might say, "It's fuzzy," or "It sits still a long time." Any detail is okay, but no repeats are allowed. More details can be added to someone else's observation, however. For example, though someone may have said, "It's fuzzy," another person can say "Its fuzz is brown."

Optional: Pick one player to record what each of you notices.

4. Continue taking turns in the same order until only one player is able to make a new observation. The last person to share a specific observation about the spider is the most aware.

Has your spider had a mathematical examination? If not, you may want to be a math doctor and look closely to discover its physical condition!

Math Doctor

What to Do:

Use the tools and materials listed to give your spider a thorough examination. Like a real doctor, you can jot down your findings.

Anatomy Checklist: How many legs does your spider have? How many body sections? What other parts can you see? Does it have eyes? How many? You might find it helpful to use the magnifying lens to answer these questions.

Size: How big is your spider? Compare it to the other small objects you've collected. What is bigger or smaller than the spider? What is the same size as your spider? Are all of its legs the same size?

Color: How many colors can you find on your spider? Try to match the colors on your spider with colors in your crayon box. Make color marks on your paper for each spider color you find.

Web Building: If your spider is the type that builds webs, use the ruler to measure its web. How big is it? How long does it take to make a web? Use your watch to find out! Watching your spider build a web can be a time-consuming challenge. Then again, it may be a good excuse for staying up late. "Mom, how can I go to bed now? My spider is still spinning its web!"

You will need:

- ✔ a spider
- ✔ a magnifying lens
- ✔ a pencil and some paper
- ✔ a variety of small objects, such as dried beans, pennies, or coins
- ✔ a box of crayons
- ✔ a watch
- ✔ a ruler

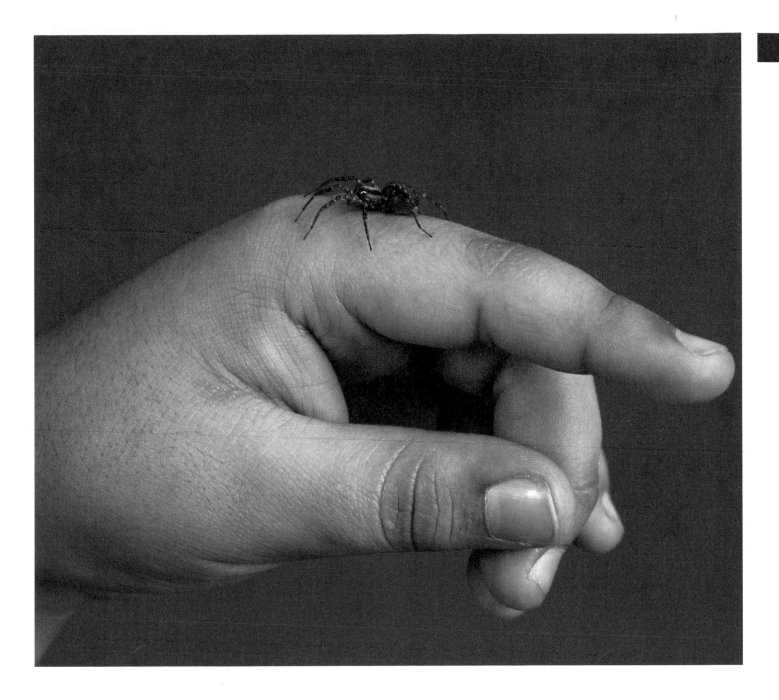

When you look at spiders up close, they seem to be dressed in high fashion. The female American black widow dresses in a lovely jet-black suit with a striking red patch on her underside. The cardinal jumping spider wears a bright velvety jumpsuit with furry black leggings. Picture your favorite spiders on giant billboards advertising spider fashion. Can you imagine your spider as a top fashion model? Well, imagine no more. Make your own mini-billboard with your spider as the model.

Fashionable Spiders

You will need:

✔ a spider
✔ paper
✔ pencil
✔ crayons or colored pencils
✔ magnifying lens

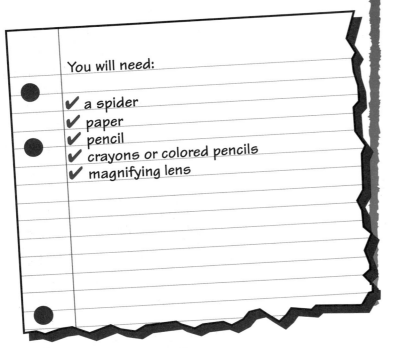

What to Do:

Follow the directions below to produce your work of art.

Fly with Your Eyes: Using the magnifying lens, pretend you are a spy plane zooming over the spider. Carefully examine its shapes, parts, and other details, such as colors and textures.

Snapshot: Make some quick, simple sketches of the different things that you notice, such as the shape of the spider's body or where its legs fit onto its body.

Value Your Curiosity: If questions such as, "What is that thing called?" pop into your brain, write them down next to your drawings. Questions are well worth collecting, because they can lead to further discoveries.

Almost There . . . : Before making the final picture, do some fast sketches of the basic shape of the spider. This will help you experiment with the picture before working on the fine details.

Bigger than Life: Drawing a spider as tiny as it is in real life is hard to do—and hard to look at! It's easier to include small details when you make your billboard big.

Art Show: Be proud of your creation. Display your billboard along your driveway, on your hedroom door, or on the family fridge.

Do you have any questions about spiders? Here are some questions that kids in my town asked:

Do spiders have teeth? Why do they have eight legs? How many different kinds of spiders are there?

Are spiders smart? Do they have their own language? What do they do when it rains? How far can they jump? How long do they live? How do they react to heat? How do they react to oil? How do they react to light and dark?

Do spiders eat bugs? Do they eat each other? How much do they eat? How long does it take for them to eat? Do they eat anything that flies into their web? What are their enemies? How long does it take a spider to build a web?

How do you tell a male from a female? How many babies can spiders have in one year?

Where do spiders go in the winter? Do spiders hibernate?

Why do black widows have an hourglass on their stomach? Will a black widow eat its babies? Is there such a thing as a mommy longlegs?

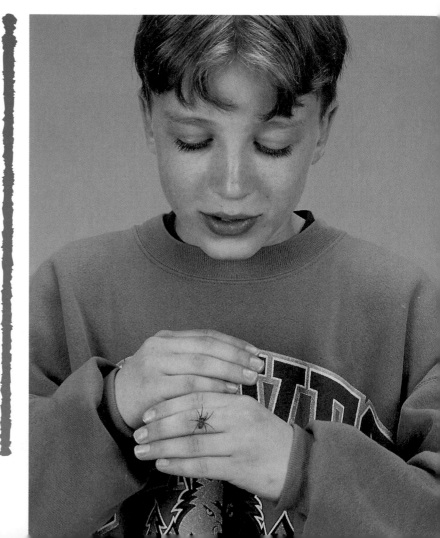

Are you ready to investigate great mysteries? Are you prepared to peer into the unknown? If you are, all you need to do is hold on to a spider question. Is there something you really wonder about spiders? Yes! Well, let that question lead you on an exploration. Below are some tips for curious spiderologists.

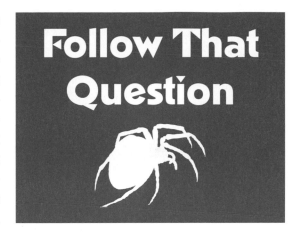

Follow That Question

—**Scrutinize:** Could you answer your question through closer observation? For example, if you wondered, "Do spiders have eyes?" do you think you could find eyes by looking at a spider through a magnifying lens?

—**Find an Expert:** Do you know a bug expert? Perhaps a local gardener, park naturalist (someone who knows about a park's plants and animals), or college instructor can give you a hand. Advice may be only a phone call away.

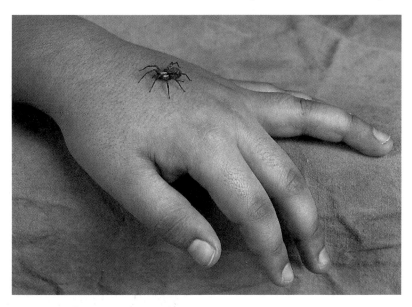

—**Research:** Other spiderologists (more properly called arachnologists) may have explored your question already. Perhaps the answer to your question can be found in a book. It might even be in this one. If you don't find the answer in this book, look at some other books. If that doesn't work, you may need to experiment—read on.

—**Experiment:** Questions often lead to experiments. What would happen if . . .? Could you answer your question with an experiment? The chapter called Kid Experiments on page 38 has stories about experiments conducted by other bold spiderologists. They may inspire you to roll up your sleeves and set up your very own experiment.

Look at this spider. Can you find eyes, antennae, or fangs? Can you find legs, wings, or stingers? Does the spider have any parts that you have or don't have?

Model Spider

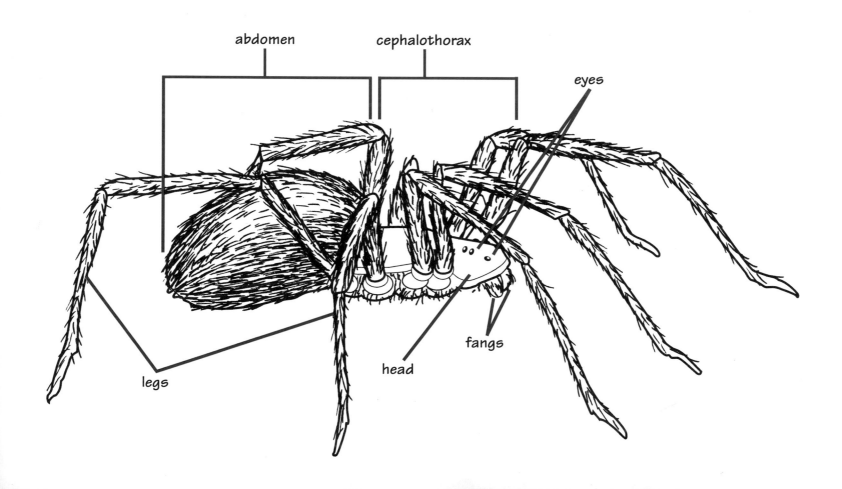

abdomen   cephalothorax

eyes

legs

head

fangs

Take a look inside this spider. Can you
discover lungs, a stomach, or a heart?

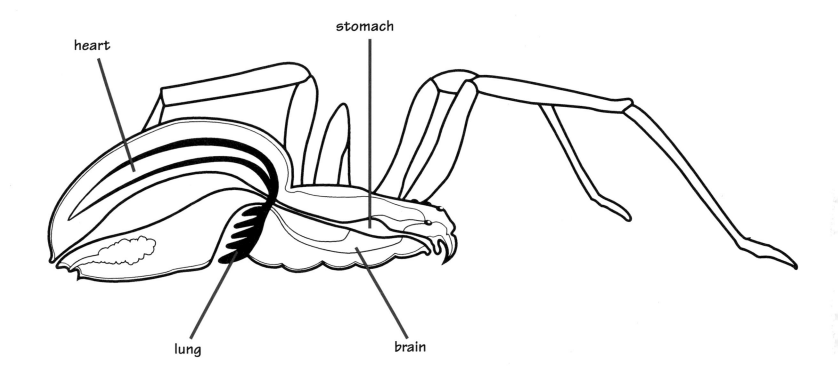

What is quieter than a mouse, but as fierce as a cat? What sheds its skin like a cricket, but has more legs than a grasshopper? What makes a cocoon like a moth, but has fangs like a rattlesnake? Would you believe . . . a spider?

What Is It?

Spiders are similar to all these animals, but their closest relatives are horseshoe crabs, scorpions, and ticks. If you have looked closely at spiders, you may have counted their eight legs and two body parts. The bodies of all spiders are divided into two sections: the **cephalothorax** (seh-fuh-luh-THOR-ax) and the **abdomen.** A spider's head and legs are attached to the cephalothorax. The abdomen is usually narrow where it meets the cephalothorax, which makes spiders look like they have thin waists.

All spiders belong to a larger group of animals called **arachnids** (a-RACK-nidz). All adult arachnids have eight legs and two body parts. Arachnids do not have antennae.

Arachnids are part of an even bigger group of animals called **arthropods.** *Arthro* means "joint" and *pod* means "foot." All arthropods have jointed feet. Centipedes, crayfish, insects, and crabs are all arthropods and distant cousins of the spider.

Check out your spider and your spider billboard. Does your spider fit the description of an arachnid and an arthropod?

Arthropods are creatures with pairs of jointed legs. The animals below are arthropods.

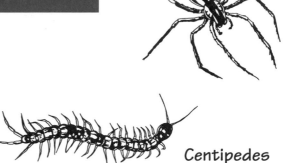

Spiders

Centipedes

Crayfish

Insects

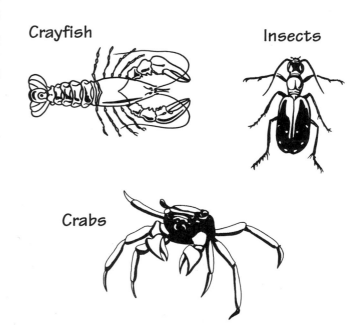

Crabs

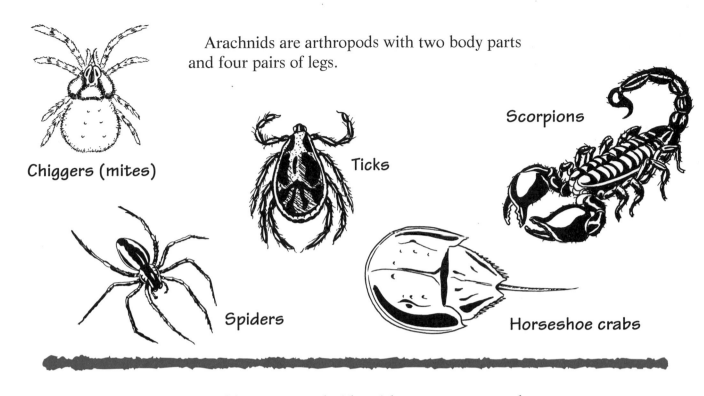

Arachnids are arthropods with two body parts and four pairs of legs.

Chiggers (mites)

Ticks

Scorpions

Spiders

Horseshoe crabs

Spiders are arachnids with an unsegmented abdomen that spin silk.

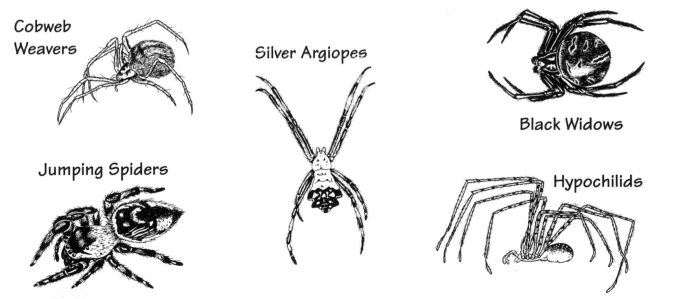

Cobweb Weavers

Silver Argiopes

Black Widows

Jumping Spiders

Hypochilids

Each language has its own word for spiders. In Maori the word for spider is *pua-werewere*. In Norwegian it's *edderkop*. In French it's *araignée*. So is it called a *puawerewere, edderkop, araignée,* or spider? To avoid using all these names, scientists have created a worldwide system of naming all living things. Whether you live in New Zealand, Norway, or France, there is only one scientific name for each **species,** or kind, of spider.

Puawerewere, Edderkop . . . Say What?

Latin and Greek, the ancient languages of Rome and Greece, are used in creating scientific names. Most kids know a few scientific names because dinosaurs have been named by scientists. For example, the name *Megalosaurus* is made up of the Greek words *mega* (great) and *saurus* (lizard). Impress your friends by saying the name of a common wolf spider, *Lycosa gulosa* (*lycos* is Greek for "wolf" and *gulos* is Latin for "gluttonous" or "piggy").

All spiders are **predators**, or hunters of other animals. The animals they catch for food are their **prey**. Spiders knock out their prey with poison, or tie them up in silk. Then they inject a special juice into them. Within a few seconds, this juice digests, or turns into liquid, part of the prey. The spider then uses its fangs to drink the liquid animal. The spider keeps injecting juice and sipping it back up until dinner is finished. Some spiders have teeth that they use to mash even the toughest parts of their prey—like the skin. This allows them to drink every last bit of their meal. Other spiders just sip until all that is left of their prey is empty skin.

Deadly Drinkers

bite to kill 300 mice!

After a spider sucks up its liquefied prey, this food is further digested in the spider's midgut. The midgut fills much of the abdomen and holds large amounts of food. This is probably one reason why spiders can live for months without eating.

A spider's heart is located in its abdomen. This powerful organ pumps food-rich blood throughout a spider's body. The heartbeat of a tarantula is 30 to 40 beats per minute. The heartbeat of smaller spiders is over 100 beats per minute, similar to the pulses of most kids.

Most spiders use poison to knock out their prey. Only 30—of more than 30,000 species of spiders in the world—have poison strong enough to harm people. The majority of these harmful spiders live in the hot parts of the planet, such as tropical rain forests. The most dangerous spiders are the ctenid spiders of South America. Unlike the black widow, these spiders are very aggressive and will attack creatures larger than themselves, even people. One species of ctenid spider injects enough poison in a single

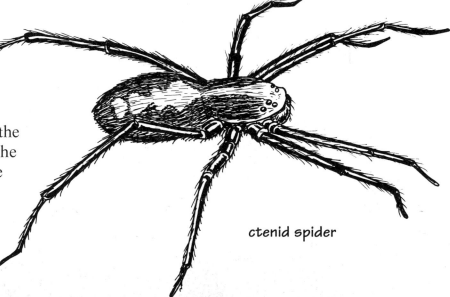

ctenid spider

Amazing Architects

To catch dinners, most spiders use traps made of silk, called webs. You can probably find a wide variety of webs on a tour of your local spiderwebs. The best known spiderweb is the orb web, made by spiders called orb weavers. This web has an outside frame, which is usually attached to branches or stems. Threads run from the frame to the center of the web—similar to spokes on the wheel of a bicycle. The number of spokes varies from 18 to 60, depending on the type of spider making the web. Over these spokes, the orb weaver lays down a spiral silk track covered with drops of glue to catch prey. From the hub (center) of this circle of silk, the spider can easily get to all parts of the web. To reach insects trapped on the glue drops, the spider merely walks on the non-sticky side of the web. This effective trap may be built in as little as half an hour.

orb weaver

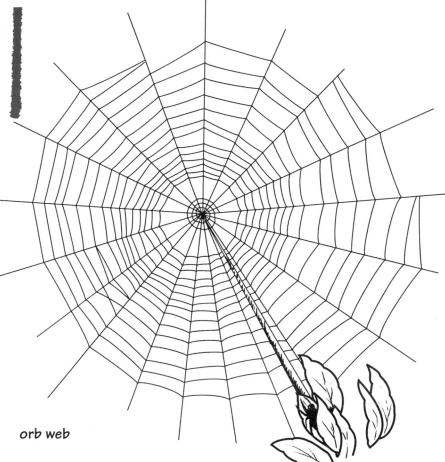

orb web

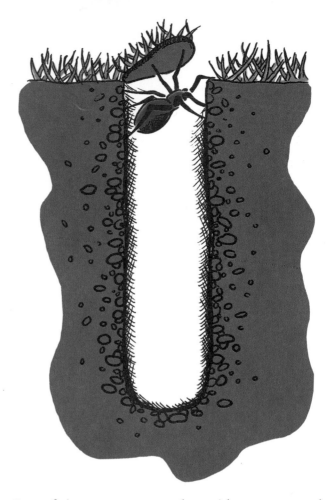

A type of web you might find outside on the lawn is the funnel trap web of the American grass spider. A funnel trap has a flat sheet of woven silk that covers the ground. Then, on one edge, there is a silk tunnel where the spider hides. Above the sheet are silk lines, which are nearly invisible in full sunlight. Flying insects that crash into these threads tumble onto the sheet and are snatched by the waiting spider.

Sheetweb-weaving spiders hide under silken sheets that are attached to branches or grass blades. The sheets may bulge upward to make domes or downward to make bowls. If an insect gets tangled in the sheet, the spider bites it and pulls it through to the underside.

You have probably seen irregular-shaped cob-webs inside houses or in rock crevices. These are made by house spiders, daddy longlegs, and black widows.

One of the most spectacular spider structures is easiest to overlook. Hidden on the ground are the little hinged doors that open to the burrows of trap-door spiders. The spider sits in its silk-lined tunnel with its door slightly open, waiting for tasty insect dinners to walk past. When an insect is within range, the spider reaches out and pulls it into the tunnel to eat it. Trap-door spiders can be found in southern parts of Europe and North America, but they are most abundant in tropical areas.

Not all spiders use webs to catch food. Spiders find their dinner in a variety of interesting ways. Some **camouflage** (KAH-muh-flazh) themselves, or blend in with their surroundings. Some crab spiders are the color of flower petals (like the crab spider below). These spiders sit on flowers and wait with outstretched legs for bees, butterflies, or other flower visitors. Crab spiders may also be the color of bark. These spiders wait on tree trunks for their

Unusual Hunters

prey. Crab spiders are invisible to their prey until it is too late—and the prey is caught in the spider's strong legs.

Free-roaming hunters, such as wolf spiders, use the many hairs that cover their bodies to tune in to the vibrations, or movements, of prey. They can even sense the buzzing wings of a fly. Wolf spiders are named after wolves because when seen in large numbers, they appear to be working together. But unlike wolves, wolf spiders do not hunt in packs.

Jumping spiders have strong jumping legs and a keen sense of sight. On the front of a jumping spider's head are two small eyes with two large eyes between them. On top of its head are another four eyes. Having eight eyes is not unusual for a spider, but few have eyes as specialized as these alert hoppers. The small eyes on the front are good for spotting movement, and the large eyes help the spider take a closer look. If it sees tasty-looking prey, the spider stalks it like a cat and tries to pounce on it. (The jumping spider on the next page has caught a cicada.) The eyes on top of the spider alert the spider to birds and other predators that might eat it!

Fisher spiders rest on leaves or water plants, waiting for insects to fall into the water. Like skaters, fisher spiders dash across the water's

surface to catch the struggling creatures.

The bola spider uses a silken thread and a gob of sticky glue to "fish" for moths! Resting on a branch, bolas give off a smell similar to the mating scent of the scodoptera moth. Male moths fly toward this smell looking for a mate. The bola spider waits until a moth comes close enough, and then swings its goo ball. When struck, the moth is stuck fast, and the spider climbs down the line to eat it. Bola spiders may catch two or three moths a night using this scent trap and lasso.

Most likely your parents have told you it is improper to spit. Not so for spitting spiders. These spiders spit a gluey goop at their prey. This goop glues the catch to the ground, allowing the spider to eat it.

Quick Snacks

Though spiders are often seen as bloodthirsty creatures, they too have to be careful so they are not eaten by other animals. Many spiders try to avoid predators by hiding out in silk tunnels at the edge of their webs or by dropping from the webs when they are disturbed. Some spiders, such as Cyclosa spiders, use camouflage. With a suit that looks like the pattern of bird droppings, a Cyclosa spider blends in perfectly with the bits of dead insect parts attached to its web. Some species of wolf spiders build tunnels to hide in, and they plug the entrance when predators come near. Micranthena spiders are covered with spines, which are believed to make them safe from birds and lizards.

Many a spider has escaped a close call by dropping a leg grabbed by a predator, the same way that a lizard discards its tail. Growing spiders can develop a new leg, but full-grown spiders of most species are unable to replace a lost leg.

Spiders make good baby food, especially for the **larvae,** or young, of certain wasps. After paralyzing a spider with a sting, the spider wasp might drag the spider to a hole. There the wasp lays its eggs on the still-living spider, then plugs the exit. When the young wasps hatch, they feed on the live spider until it dies. Few spiders are safe from these attacks. Even tarantulas are no match for the large wasp called the tarantula hawk (shown stinging a tarantula on the next page). The tarantula tries to defend itself once it is stung by the wasp, but it is unable to move. Mud dauber wasps are also serious spider hunters. A single female may collect as many as three hundred spiders in one summer.

Although wasps are major enemies, the biggest threat to spiders is other spiders. Both the cryptic jumping spider and the pirate spider invade other webs and attack the spiders there. Even the fragile-looking daddy longlegs may eat its eight-legged neighbors.

Like other animals, male and female spiders need to mate to create young spiders. During mating, males must get close enough to females to deliver sperm, or male sex cells, to the female so she can **fertilize** her eggs. When the eggs are fertilized, they are able to grow into young spiders.

According to folk myth, mating can be deadly for the male black widow. The story goes that the male is munched like candy by the female spider just after she mates. That's why she is called a "widow." In reality, the male black widow usually leaves the female's web safely.

Entertaining Dates

Uninvited males, however, may be seen as snack food to some female spiders. But a male of the same species that gives the right mating signals is usually rewarded with both mating and freedom. A male grass spider plucks the web of the female grass spider to announce himself. Male jumping spiders usually perform a dance routine to win the female's favor, and male nursery web spiders offer dead bugs. Despite the good fortunes of most male spiders, a few, such as the pallid orb weaver, will probably die during mating.

Some spiders, such as the male wolf spider, wave their **pedipalps** before mating. These organs are next to a spider's fangs and look like another pair of legs. You can tell which spiders are mature males by looking at their pedipalps—they are swollen at the tips. Inside each bulblike tip, the male carries sperm. During mating, which may take several hours, the male deposits his sperm in a special sac inside the female. The female stores the sperm here until she is ready to fertilize her eggs.

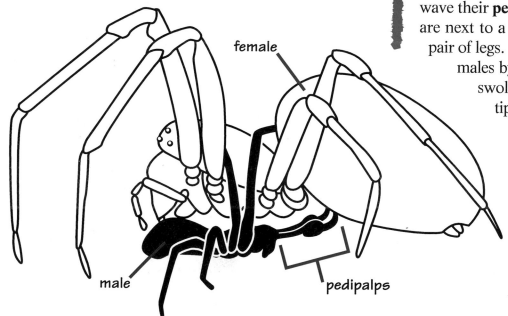

female

male

pedipalps

A female spider spins a cocoon to lay her eggs in. These egg sacs may be tied to stems, hidden in folded leaves, or hung in the spider's web. A single cocoon may hold as many as 2,000 eggs. No wonder there are spiders everywhere! During the next 2 months, the female spider may make another five cocoons. But each cocoon will have fewer eggs than the last one.

Spider Kids

that they mate, but females may live a year or two. Some, like female tarantulas, may live to be over 20 years old!

It takes only a few weeks for most spider eggs to hatch. The young spiderlings hatch inside the safety of the cocoon but don't look quite like spiders yet. They have short legs and are hairless, but grow quickly and soon **molt,** or shed their skins. Spiders, like other animals with hard external skeletons, must shed their armorlike skins in order to grow. Imagine you had tight-fitting clothes that were hard as a knight's armor. As you grew, your clothes wouldn't stretch. From time to time, you would need new armor.

After the young spiders have molted, they chew their way out of the cocoon. Looking like miniature adults, these spiderlings are big enough to catch prey and inject poison. They will grow and molt several more times during the next few months. A spider may molt 3 to 10 times during its life. It is easy to find discarded skins in spiderwebs.

After the spiderlings molt for the last time, they are ready to mate. Males die during the season

Spectacular Spinners

Spiders are not the only creatures that make silk. Animals such as caterpillars and caddis flies make silk too, but few animals have as many uses for it as spiders. After crawling out of their cocoons, many species of spiderlings find new homes by actually taking off into the air. This flight is called ballooning, though it's more like "kiting." With its tail end poking up in the air, the spider releases long threads of silk. When this silk is caught in a breeze, the tiny spider is lifted up into the air and carried to new hunting grounds.

Ballooning spiders may travel hundreds of miles and reach heights of 20,000 feet or more! Although these spiders are mostly at the mercy of the winds, some have been seen gathering the silk threads to steer.

Like rock climbers, spiders can lower themselves on lines from webs, branches, and other high places. Unlike rock climbers, they make the line themselves and lay it down wherever they go. If a spider falls off a branch, it is caught by this safety line. To return to the branch, it just climbs back up the silk thread. Most spiders make these drag lines. Watch a spider and see if you can see it attaching this safety silk as it moves about.

When most spiders molt, they retreat to a hidden spot and weave a special molting chamber. Other spiders make threads to hang from while molting. Hibernating spiders are often found in silken sacs. The water spider uses silk to build a bell-shaped air chamber underwater, where it stores air carried down from above. In this underwater home, the spider raises its young and eats its meals.

Silk is produced in glands found in the **spinnerets,** or silk-making organs. Three pairs of spinnerets are found on the tip of a spider's abdomen. Spiders can produce different types of silk, such as cocoon silk, sticky silk, and dragline silk from a variety of silk glands.

Some spiders are silk recyclers. Certain orb weavers eat their old web before building a new one. These spiders will create new silk using recycled substances from the digested silk meal.

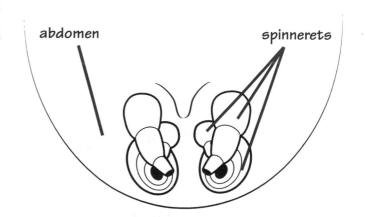

abdomen

spinnerets

Students at El Portal Elementary School, my local school in California, wove their spider questions into some answer-catching experiments. As you check out their explorations, maybe you'll get ideas for tests of your own!

What Can a Spider Climb?

Nalani noticed that her smaller spider couldn't climb out of a plastic container, but a larger faster spider could. Her spider did, however, climb up her partner Ali, the side of a wooden bookshelf, and a book. When the girls placed the spider on a computer screen, it jumped off, and they thought it was afraid. What else do you think spiders can climb?

What Will a Spider Eat?

Candice and Elizabeth dropped two live fruit flies into a container with their spider. The spider ate the flies within a few minutes. Next, they gave the spider some leaves to munch on, but it left the leaves untouched. When they put a cricket in with a spider, it wrapped its legs around the cricket but did not eat it. Candice and Elizabeth watched for 15 minutes, and the spider moved away from the cricket without eating it.

Would a spider eat another spider? Carefully, the girls transferred their spider into the web of a smaller one. The little spider ran away and hid in a box on the shelf, while the bigger spider settled itself on the web. It just hung upside down and did not move for 15 minutes. The girls thought that the bigger spider liked to eat bugs, but it wouldn't eat big ones like crickets or other spiders. What do you think spiders might eat?

How Do Spiders React to Oil?

Rico and Nicholas noticed oil on the ground beneath cars and wondered what spiders would do if they came across some. Would the oil trap them? They dripped some 3-in-1 oil on a sheet of plastic and let a spider roam across the sheet. Nicholas and Rico did five tests, using a different spider each time. The spiders all acted as if they didn't know the oil was there until they stepped in it. When the spiders touched the oil, they backed away. The boys figured that the spiders backed away from the oil because it was sticky.

How Do Spiders React to Loud Sounds?

What if a spider built its web next to the speaker on your CD player? Would it like the tunes, or would it move to a more peaceful location?

Carroll, Kyle, and Alex loaded a Walkman with some rock music and then played it at high volume near a spider housed in a plastic container.

This is what happened:

Test #1:

The spider seemed scared at first. It tried to get away, but then stopped its escape attempt.

Test #2:

It tried to escape the entire time.

Test #3, using a wolf spider:

It looked as if it were trying to attack the headphones.

Carroll, Kyle, and Alex decided that spiders do react to sound but then get used to it. Do you agree?

How Do Spiders Act Together?

Nick wondered what would happen if he put two daddy longlegs spiders together. Would they eat each other? A half hour after being in the same container, both daddy longlegs were alive. They also began making webs. Before the end of the day, Nick added another spider to the two in the container. The next morning, they were all hanging out near each other on their webs, which were connected. Nick thought that even if daddy longlegs were starved, they would hunt together with other daddy longlegs. But other kinds of spiders might eat each other. What do you think? Have you ever seen daddy longlegs hanging out together in your house?

How Do Different Kinds of Spiders Get Along?

To discover how a wolf spider and a daddy long-legs would act with each other, Leann, Melissa, and Elizabeth placed one of each kind in a large pan with a clear sheet of plastic for a lid. The daddy longlegs wandered about the inside wall of the round pan like a horse going around a race-track. The wolf spider settled next to one section of wall and stayed there. Several times, the daddy longlegs encountered the wolf spider, and this is what happened:

Test #1: The daddy longlegs crawled over the wolf spider.

Test #2: The daddy longlegs put one leg on the wolf spider, the wolf spider struck at it, and both moved away from each other.

Test #3: The daddy longlegs climbed on top of the wolf spider, then the wolf spider chased after it.

Test #4: After the daddy longlegs put its leg on the back of the wolf spider, the wolf spider stuck its leg out.

The spiders had several more run-ins, and basically the same thing happened each time. They would touch each other and back off. The girls thought that the daddy longlegs was mostly bothering the wolf spider and causing the wolf spider to chase it. What do you think?

How Fast Does a Spider Go?

Katelyn and Alison had seen some spiders move pretty fast and wondered exactly how fast they were traveling. To measure spider speed, they constructed a racetrack between two yardsticks. Each of six daddy longlegs was released between the yardsticks, and the girls recorded the time it took to travel from one end to the other. This is how long it took each spider to go one yard:

Spider #1: 43 seconds
Spider #2: 14 seconds
Spider #3: 46 seconds
Spider #4: 58 seconds
Spider #5: 40 seconds
Spider #6: 130 seconds

It would take 2½ days to travel a mile at the speed of the slowest spider. On the other hand, it would take a mere 7 hours to go a mile at the speed of the fastest spider. How long does it take you to travel a mile? Alison and Katelyn think some kinds of spiders are faster than others. Do you think you can beat their fastest crawler with another kind of spider? Go for it!

Beat the Heat

Imagine waiting for lunch in the smoldering sun of a hot tropical day. That is what many spiders must do as they lie on their webs in wait for flying food. How do they beat the heat?

One of the largest tropical spiders is the golden web spider, or *Nephila clavipes.* It builds a web as big as a hula hoop and strong enough to catch small birds, which sometimes get entangled in the silk. These webs are often built in open areas, where they get blasted by the heat of the midday sun. Michael and Barbara Robinson, scientists at the Smithsonian Tropical Research Institute in Panama, wondered what the spiders did to avoid getting overheated. Did they change their positions to avoid sunlight? Did they move out of the sunlight?

Many golden web spiders had built webs along a road near the research institute. Using a compass, the Robinsons measured the direction each web was facing. They also calculated the slope, or tilt, of each web. All this information was recorded before they watched the spiders' reactions to sunlight. Using a movie camera, they documented the actions of the spiders as the sun changed position. They also experimented by shining light from a mirror onto spiders that were in the shade. They filmed the spiders' reactions to the light from the mirror, too.

For two months, they filmed the actions of spiders in 49 webs. Then Robinson and Robinson watched the film in slow motion and took notes on the movements of the spiders. They compared the spiders' movements to the position of the light. As they examined their data, it became clear that golden web spiders move their bodies into different positions as the direction of the light shining on them changes.

A spider often points the tip of its abdomen at the sun and points its head toward the web. This way only the end of the abdomen gets full sunlight. Positions like this help the spiders keep most of their body surface out of direct sunlight. To see how this works, hold a book with its cover facing a light. Now turn the book so that the spine faces the light. Does the book get exposed to less light when just the spine is facing the light? Though golden web spiders aren't as flat as books, the tail end of their abdomen is smaller in surface area than their backside.

When the Robinsons flashed light off a mirror at the webs, the spiders changed position every time the angle of the mirror was changed. On hot summer days, it might be helpful to remember the actions of these tropical spiders. What could you do to stay cooler in the hot sun?

Space Spiders

In 1948 a German spiderologist, H. M. Peters, asked a friend of his to help him change the time when garden spiders build their webs. Peters had been studying web building, but didn't like having to get up early in the morning when garden spiders do their construction (2 A.M. to 5 A.M.). His friend, P. N. Witt, gave the spiders a dose of a drug called amphetamine to stimulate them to spin their webs earlier. Rather than building their webs earlier, the spiders spun webs that were irregular. They made webs with unevenly spaced spokes of different lengths. Witt became curious about the effects of drugs on spiders and gave them other drugs such as caffeine, which is found in coffee, chocolate, and cola. The more caffeine he gave them, the stranger their webs became. These drugs were definitely not helpful to spiders. Later, Witt and other scientists sent spiders into space on Skylab, a space station built by the United States in the 1970s. Up in space, there is no gravity to hold things down, a condition called zero gravity. Witt and his partners wondered how zero gravity would affect the web-building spiders. To many people's surprise, the spiders built normal webs despite the complete weightlessness!

Mysteries of a Backyard Buddy

Although this is the end of the book, it is only the beginning of spiderology. Remember those questions you asked? Are all of them answered? Maybe this book is too little to answer everyone's spider wonderings. Or perhaps there is still so much to learn about spiders that it could take centuries to answer the questions we already have. Maybe no one else has ever thought of your question before. It could be up to you to try and answer it!

Easily answered questions are like a neatly spun web, while challenging mysteries are like a tangled mess of silken threads. Consider your tangled questions once more and picture the wild adventures they could lead to. Pick up the thread and follow it to the point of knowing. Below are some questions that kids from El Portal may still be unraveling at this very moment.

Why does a black widow have an hourglass on its stomach?

Are spiders smart?

Where do spiders go when it rains?

Why do they have eight legs?

Where do spiders go in winter?

Glossary

abdomen: the tail-end section of a spider

arachnids: a group of animals, including spiders, that have eight legs and two body parts

arthropods: a large group of animals with jointed legs and segmented bodies

camouflage: a way of disguising something by making it blend in with its surroundings

cephalothorax: the front section of a spider, where the head and legs are located

fertilize: the coming together of sperm and egg to create new life

larvae: the wormlike young of some types of insects

molt: to shed skin

pedipalps: leglike organs near the mouth of a spider. The pedipalps of an adult male spider carry sperm.

predator: an animal that hunts and kills other animals

prey: an animal eaten by other animals

species: a group of animals with common traits, especially the ability to create young like themselves

spinnerets: organs where silk is made

Index

About the Author

For over twenty years, Michael Elsohn Ross has taught visitors to Yosemite National Park about the park's wildlife and geology. Mr. Ross, his wife, Lisa (a nurse who served nine seasons as a ranger-naturalist), and their son, Nick, have led other families on wilderness expeditions from the time Nick learned to crawl. Mr. Ross studied conservation of natural resources at the University of California/Berkeley, with a minor in entomology (the study of insects). His other books for children include the Naturalist's Apprentice series, also published by Carolrhoda Books.

Mr. Ross makes his home on a bluff above the wild and scenic Merced River, at the entrance to Yosemite. His backyard garden is a haven for rolypolies, crickets, snails, worms, spiders, ladybugs, and a myriad of other intriguing critters.